FAULTDANCING

FAULTDANCING

William Pitt Root

University of Pittsburgh Press

Published by the University of Pittsburgh Press, Pittsburgh, Pa., 15260
Copyright © 1986, William Pitt Root
Feffer and Simons, Inc., London
Manufactured in the United States of America

Library of Congress Cataloging in Publication Data

Root, William Pitt, 1941–
  Faultdancing.

  (Pitt poetry series)
  I. Title. II. Series.
PS3568.O66F38 1986   811'.54   85-40858
ISBN 0-8229-3530-9
ISBN 0-8229-5380-3 (pbk.)

I want to thank the editors of the following anthologies and periodicals in which these poems originally appeared: *Big River News* ("Song of the Dawncock," "Song of Levels," "Song of Salt and the Gale," and "Song of the Windwalker"); *Chicago Review* ("The Glass House"); *Columbia: A Magazine of Poetry & Prose* ("Blue Lake Dream"); *Floating Island* ("Dreaming the Shark, Waking the Dream"); *Jeopardy* ("Temperance Poems"); *Malahat Review* ("Song from the Surface of the Earth"); *The Nation* ("Song of an Eye's Opening" and "Song of a Hawk's Glance"); *Nimrod* ("Fireclock"); *Poetry* ("Half Shift," "Leopard Lost in High Snow," and "Song"); *Prickly Pear Quarterly* ("As If" and "Lunar Phase"); *Quarterly West* ("Anamax Open Pit" and "Sweat"); *Slackwater Review* ("Like Hills. Like Water"); *Southeast Arts Journal* ("At the Foot of a Holy Mountain" and "Near Little River Cemetery"); *Spoor* ("Little Song of Patience" and "Song Altering All"); *Three Rivers Poetry Journal* ("Wanderer's Dream of Fire"); *Vanderbilt Review* ("November Field"); *Writers Forum* ("Opening the Season"); and *Yarrow* ("Inference from the Eyes of a Hawk," "Song of the Consolation," "To Build a House Upon the Rock," and "To Walk Across").

Thanks also to Graywolf Press which first published "The Anonymous Welcome" under its previous title, "A Journey South," in its chapbook series; to Mississippi Mud Press, which published most of the "Feast of Light" section as *7 Mendocino Songs*; to 4 Zoas Press, which published "Fireclock" as a chapbook; and to Ray Rice (Mendocino, California), who based his film, *Faces*, upon poems in this book.

Finally, thanks to the National Endowment for the Arts whose aid in the form of a grant was invaluable.

The publication of this book is supported by grants from the National Endowment for the Arts in Washington, D.C., a Federal agency, and the Pennsylvania Council on the Arts.

*This book is for Lana, as promised, at last,
and for Hans Taaibosch
and Laurens van der Post—light-bearers all.*

"Must man char to limn?"
—St. Augustine

"A poet is the thief of fire"
—Rimbaud

Other Works by William Pitt Root

Invisible Guests, 1984
In the World's Common Grasses, 1981
Reasons for Going It on Foot, 1981
Coot and Other Characters, 1977
Striking the Dark Air for Music, 1973
The Storm and Other Poems, 1969

Chapbooks
The Unbroken Diamond: Nightletter to the Mujahideen, 1983
Fireclock, 1981
A Journey South, 1977
7 Mendocino Songs, 1977

Translation
Selected Odes of Pablo Neruda, 1986

Editor
Timesoup: Poetry and Art by Young Alaskans, 1980
Whataworld, Whataworld: Poetry by Young People in Galveston Schools, 1973

Collaborations
For a Magician, with Ray Price, 1975 (film)
The Woman and the Butterflyman, with Ray Price, 1974 (film)
The Port of Galveston, photographs by Richard Tichich, Betty Tichich, and Jean-Claude Marchant; text by William Pitt Root, 1974

CONTENTS

CONTENTS

FAULTDANCING

WANDERER'S DREAM OF FIRE

Looking for one place
I am not on my way away from
as I enter, where can I go?

My mind blows white as snow
with memories melting as they form,
one memory the sure knowledge

that memory is a lie time
tells itself, as a storyteller
babbles on, alone, to his fire.

> *Where have I been?—Becoming*
> *the fire to whom*
> *some stranger speaks, fire that warms*
> *and swaddles him in shadows as he sleeps.*

In that sleep he dreams of being fire.

This is his tale.

1. The Anonymous Welcome

THE ANONYMOUS WELCOME

1. First Day

In the noon glare
of flat houses
and clay faces
we jounce east through
Tijuana, then hit the brakes:
Three men and a boy,
attended by a ring
of laughing girls,
teeter and rock
an old icebox
across the vacant street.
They do not look at us.
Gringos, turistas.
There will be cold
milk for the mornings,
chilled cervezas
for the nights—
but now there is fun,
there is this
to be done.
We wait.

Across the rough
ceramic of this land
fired by summer sun,
we pass an afternoon
of lowered windows
with avocados, oranges,
Coke, aware
how our own tongue
becomes slowly alien.

7

At twilight
we drive rising
into fading hills
east of a town,
curving up and up
into the gradually
cooling night,
then slowing
for the dim truck
huge ahead, square
against the stars.
Ghostbright in
the broad flood
of the truck's headlights,
a car coming down
in the wrong lane
swerves, hits
head-on,
freezes, then
all the doors
fling open
in a moment
frozen bright
as it rolls
over the edge,
slowly over
the edge,
and down.

A man is under
the trailer
wheels, trapped
at the shoulder.

He gestures
with the free hand,
slowly arches
like a mantis.
"Señor,
por favor?"

The truck's driver
is rigid
in the worn seat,
eyes straight ahead. I plead
with him to come.
He stares.
"Hombre! Hombre!"
He stares. I pull
him, wooden, from the cab,
show him the man.
Pinned to the blacktop,
from his back
he nods an apology.
The driver shrugs
and looks deep
into the fields,
walks away.

The other suddenly
is shivering. I take
his hand. It is cold.
He sees, asks a question
I don't understand.
Tears that start
in his eyes
run down my face.

A hundred yards below
the walleyed car
rumbles and gurgles.
Already it is old
as the stones
in the place
around it. The radio
still sings, remote
with mariachis
then the static
of the crickets.

There is another
lying by the road,
and he is dying.
Above one eye,
a hole the size
of an eye.
Through it stares
a globe of brain, blind,
weeping slow blood.
He is curled
like a broken doll,
breathing
like broken machinery.

He is dying
in his shirt
bright as the moon.
There is no one
for him. *Father*
I begin
but the word
breaks in my throat.

10

My own father died
like this, alone
beside the road.
I make a prayer
of silence
for this stranger,
touch his hand.
I am alone.

These fields,
they reek
with raw manure.
It mixes in the wind
with sweet smells
of cooling grass,
deep as the earth,
disturbingly green.
The sky's on fire
with stars
and the last crickets
of twilight
tick
like mad clocks.

Cars stop. Now
others walk up
from the town, pass
by as if it
were a market
commenting
upon this one,
that one, brushing
flies away
with their hands,

their brilliant
teeth and eyes
transformed
by the moon.

The one
beneath the truck
is miraculously free. He squats.
His unshaven face
is dark with pain
above the white
starched shirt.
And he is drunk.
He does not turn to look
toward the other.

We drive on
into the dark gorges
north of the desert,
slowly, my wife and I,
watching for miles
the approach
of each car as we wind
toward each other
and pass each other
into the night.

2. Second Day
Next morning
the desert is magnificent,
each bright trace of life
fierce and welcome.

Simple stones are brilliant
where flowers of plastic
marking roadside graves
bleach and warp.
The farthest buttes are clear,
wavering above the horizon
like ships hovering
upon the lake of heat.
Within a hundred miles
the floor of the desert
flattens to a vanishing point.
Cactus disappear
and the flash
of the occasional rats.
The horizon is an unbroken ring.

By late afternoon,
the Gulf of California
is a glittering blue desert
bulging beyond the white one.
In the single stretch of cloud
across the coastal hills,
a gradual wheel of gulls
circles and falls.

We shower in warm water,
glad for the shade
in a room with peeling walls.
Thin pale curtains flutter
with a breeze we barely feel.
There is still the sand
as we roll with each other
in the clean smell of the sheets.

Strangers here, our kisses
have the stranger's touch
as we taste the salt of ourselves
mix with salt from the sea.

We swim, drink cervezas,
sit hours in a blue tavern
painted bright with gamefish,
haunted as the sun sets
by a man with trinkets:
crucifixes, dirty cards,
switchblade knives.
"Señor?
Señora?"

That night
we climb the stony hill
together and find at the top
a shrine for fishermen
adorned with the perennial
flowers of plastic,
strands of Christmas bulbs,
tinsel. In the cove
murmuring and twinkling
below us lies the wreckage
of four fishing boats
that come alive each day
for crews of children
and each night for rats.

Looking out over the town
housed by the burning roof
of stars, lit by the moon,
our faces turn the color
of desert stone.

14

There the stars,
there the waves of sand,
and there the curving sea
extend outward away from us forever.

Below,
the town
we've come to now.
From here
it is all simply rows
of the frailest lights,
the faint serenade
of mariachis, juke
in the tavern attended
by the frozen grins
of varnished marlins.
How can I tell you
what I would tell you
—you, whose face of obsidian
and silver is as wise,
as indecipherable,
as moonlight?

Over there
at the nearest edge
of town
in a field of light
preserved from the dark,
children still play.
Going down
on a path of stones,
the closer to them we come
the louder the anonymous
welcome of that laughter.

15

2. Idiots of Appetite

DREAMING THE SHARK,
WAKING THE DREAM

That grim hoop, hinged and toothed and terrible
jawbone from a Great White
jolting like a shock through the submarine
currents of our dream, how
harmless merely waking could render it—
unless as we dreamers wake the dream wakes too
in its black sunrise, unless the head reforms incredibly
around the yawning vacuum of that ruthless jaw
and round the body muscles to propel it through a sea
just warm enough to sustain cold blood,
a sea that surrounds and buoys it again
as again our familiar vessel passes over
while we, dazed by the sun and moon
     our spectral ship sails through, slide
from the bow given slowly into waves where we must
float half in the world or air, half in the water,
innocent of any wish that the ship veer to save us
and innocent of any wish to drown.

For by that saline light our lashes drip
we must desire our lives
     embracing and embraced by water
as we breathe, swimming, waiting, saving one coherent cry
against the first sign of the fin that slits foaming
from trough to wavetop toward us, circling,
tightening the wide rings of light. And if
     on the first pass it misses
it must return, it must remember to return,
must not fear our kicking, our thrashing half up out of water,
our seeking with blind hands across the monumental face
     for the flat eyes incapable of closure;

19

must take us, must not let go—
although we wake from our dream, it will wake,
    will hold and hold until all we can become
is solved in that single resolution
a wakeful sea shall render gaunt, reduce to one grim smile of bone
drifting the lightless sea-miles down in an abyss
    too cold, too far and dark,
for even the most relentless light's formal reflection.

This is the dream we wake to when we wake.

LEOPARD LOST IN HIGH SNOW

Here its claws grasp nothing.

      Snow like light rises
at the touch of wind and shifts: a world
is changed, and soon will change again.
Nothing here holds within that grip
designed for earth. Nothing coheres.
Tracks that were pocks an hour ago
protrude like craters now above the new
surface devised by constant wind.
Between blind sun and blinding snow
the gold-eyed cat turns, stares down its own
length where the familiar stretch of markings
expands across warm muscle, contracts
against the cold. All color and design
which hid it in its own wilderness
expose it here. It has come too far.
It snarls and is prey now to the clear
howling wind. Its rage burns
absolute and pure.

      It murders snow.

INFERENCE FROM THE EYES OF A HAWK

Before the tender glaring of these eyes
the world brightens. Must brighten.
Glows with the light of being seen.
Glows with the sheen of an immanence
          delicate as golden powder.
Air among his feathers whispers.
Blood within his veins.
For whomsoever he chooses, the air bursts red.

LIKE HILLS. LIKE WATER

Such a bull,
this one.
　　　　White
hills of deep muscle
on those shoulders ride.
All that wedge
of weight narrows
to ankles
and the ankles flare
out into hooves
flat against an earth
hard as horn. As stone.
The two halves of night
gather in its eyes.
From the cave of its skull
a world's darkness
looks out at the light.

This bull.
　　　　It is the shadow
of a terrible angel
fallen into flesh,
angered by the fall. Awful
the slow heat of such incarnate rage.
Look at the prehuman eyes
captive in their skull, eyes swelling
at the edges of that brain,
rolling like the moon.
Like hills. Like water.
And gradual muscles of the water
wrap this heaving ground. Immovable,
yet set to move.

LUNAR PHASE

3 A.M. The moonlit wash out back
runs with coyotes now.
        They cry out
teasing dogs wild and haunting the sleep
of masters with dreams hollow-eyed
as their howls, chopped by yips and barks.
But I'm not dreaming now. These letters
scrawled in the crabbed shadow of my dusty hand
speak of moving again: After a year
of Vermont and that winter paralyzed
in snow spring finally took to heart,
thawed in the fire of its grasses,
its igneous blossoms, leaves: After
a season of rocks and sunflowers
and mules in the Mediterranean, and another
where redwoods jut like columns
in that cathedral of all weathers: Then
hitching crosscountry to settle where
prickly pear edges out of the earth our Anglo
herds have overgrazed. My thoughts
are windshield landscapes. My eyes open
to the underground chiaroscuro of the coppermine
and the mantrain dropping us too far
from the mainshaft to save us from the fire
we all sniff the air for. Chutetapping—
doublejack, hook and bar, working my headlamp,
pulling the rushes of ore, blasting raises,
risking open grizzlies in 160° heat. Darkness
floating the bright rubble of stars
ends the midnight shift.

Every night, 3 A.M.,
coyotes like crazed children
and the ghosts of crazed children cry out
against the furious resistance of tame dogs
who snarl from doorsteps in the dark
while their masters sleep.
                                What dreams survive
this persistent dream of waking, eyes preferring
shades to substance, dreams
to the things dreamt of? *The ways, the ways.*

HALF SHIFT

I follow you back into town
after these hours of tension
in the canyon our last day. Your car

is sick and shakes. I follow
watching the sky darken for
twilight and a storm. Oncoming

miners headed for swingshift
in that black shaft I worked not long ago
fill the lane out of town

with headlights. Then we both notice
how the plumskin horizon
streaks yellow and green. I stop,

you stop. We gaze east
at the ripening light while
at our backs the mountains darken

and the storm comes down.
Four hours later I drive home
blind in rain while the miners

half a mile below drop their doublejacks
and drills to eat, deaf to all
disturbances from the earth above.

LEARNING PRAYER AMONG STONES

To speak to rock
is to become rock,
whose mouth
is the gradual utterance
of sand
upon tongues of water
and the wind.
Is to be blind
to the nightvoid
and dayvoid
of moon and sun.
Reflections, origin:
Eyes of the owl
deep in saguaro
in the ghost of a sea,
eyes of the iguana
set in the sparkle
of the living surf.
Deaf. Numb to the cleavages
and crumbling of self.
To not speak.
To remain
among stones
a stone.

AT THE FOOT OF A HOLY MOUNTAIN

Nothing seems more still
than this desert at night,
late, after the breezes
of twilight
establish themselves
in the chaparral.

The crickets are quiet
and the moon is silent
as a sailboat
in a children's book
here where each incarnate scrap
hunts for another,
cold glass eyes
fired by night hunger.

Webbed feet and scaled bellies
scour the rocks and sand
while wings overhead
cross and recross
the scarred face of the moon,
and all the idiots of appetite
pursue each other blindly
by the jeweled light of their jeweled eyes.

AS IF

We speak of dying as if we will live forever
to speak of it at all
in this bare forest of lies
words are, each illusion
a luminous fear
only language can secure.

Of all noise-making creatures
only we
believe this wilderness
we dare not leave and cannot harvest,
although we thresh and refine
syllables and ciphers
as if they were grain. As if.

NOVEMBER FIELD

Sunflowers nod toward the moon,
birdriddled faces glowing,
frostbright leaves
extending into darkness
above roots that analyze
     the ground, embracing stones
in the embrace which leaves them sand.

Each, once,
was instrumental to the sun.

OPENING THE SEASON

Slaughter is kinder than starvation.

Leaves lie like tobacco on the ground,
too damp to crackle warning. Throughout
the heavy air scents bleed,
and no sound comes through clear.

The natural predators are gone.

Tonight the highways will be bright
with hunters driven to the woods
by months among blind walls.

Winterfeed is scarce, too scarce.

And the woods are lit by eyes
splashes of blood will lid
against wind spilling
across the hoods and roof-racks
their split bodies are bound to.

Doors shut, trunks click, lids pop.

                                    Already
their grass-stained lips
shrink back from the teeth
against which each set of high beams
ignites the secret grin over and over.

Shell chambers gleam, slam.

These frostwhite woods burn radiant
as angels opening morning,
and everything that moves moves with care
where the innocent are stalked by the justified.

ℬ◆ Fireclock

FIRECLOCK

"Are they mountains? Are they clouds?
It's hard to tell
but when mist opens and clouds disperse
the mountains remain."
—Su Tung-p'o

1.

I wake
to the iron-dark length of a train
where everyone is sleeping. The ticket
printed on my hand
says I'm going back, going back
I don't know where. I smell breath
in the air, feel the heavy round wheels
glide on moonlit track.

Racket in my belly,
agitation in my bones.

I want to see the moon,
but this blind is padlocked.
I want to see the moon.
I step out. The aisle shines.

> *Their fingers are torches,*
> *their heads crowns of fire.*

2.

Late,
I know it's late. This kind of light's
forever—machines make it
that never sleep. I cannot
find a clock but the walls tick.
I listen, trying to hear
the wheels riding on moonlight.

35

Moon, Moon,
do you have the time?
I'm going back,
sealed in the bright air
of a train going back
I don't know where.

I wait. Nothing.
I listen. Nothing.
Moon says nothing
and I start to walk.
No land under the moon.
No stars, no sky.
Nothing seems to move
as we move
along the tracks
that can't be seen.

> *Please, the child's face says.*
> *Please, the fire hurts me.*

The engineer must know
what time it is,
where we are going.
The fire in the firebox
must be real with real shadows.
In my mind I see his face
blown by the wind. He smiles,
his eyes close. Don't sleep,
don't sleep! His head falls forward.

3.

    Going back
car after glowing car
I can't find my place again.
I run: door after door closing behind
opens before me
100 times, 1,000,
until I am too tired even to breathe.

One last door and the air
brightens with new odor
and this car opens
full of babies
hung in hammocks
in a dim green light
and as in an aquarium
the creatures here are similar
as a race of dolls.
Not one is awake,
not one smiling
or frowning.

Who is caring for the babies?

4.

    Further back
and further in the whole train
there is no one
but these children
smaller car by car
until they are infants,
froglike embryos,
the eyes blind bulges,

37

the fingers buds,
while all around
the air is green
and warm,
is heavy,
lulls.

Everything is smaller,
the locks shining
like toys. Trying
to remember about locks
I watch them shine.
When I reach to try one
my hand is a baby hand,
the lock is huge.
When I start to scream
I start to shrink.
I mustn't shrink.
I leave the locks alone
and my hands
are mine again,
mine, and trembling.

> *Please, the face says, please.*
> *And smoke curls from the lips,*
> *then flame.*

5.

Awake
I am alone, breathing
the humid breath of the sleepers,
the heavy air like ether.
I am too tired to be alone
and it is hot, too hot.

The train knows I don't like it
so it's getting hot.

Or is it fire?—
There's smoke,
smoke must mean someone,
someone is awake!

I run into the smoke
and the smoke grows thicker.
Hello? I run into the smoke
and the smoke grows hotter.
Hello? The smoke is dark,
then brightens so I see
my clothes are burning,
that light comes from
my clothes! I back up,
tear them from my skin.
Suddenly I'm ugly
in a char of rags.

6.
    I lift them up.
Their fingers are on fire,
their toes spurt flame.
I lift them up.
Their faces
are wide loud holes.
Too many! But when I
cry out, my words
feed the fire. Terror
feeds it, prayer feeds it,
it grows on air.

In this train
all eyes are sealed
in useless sleep.
In this train
what's real is fire—
children shrieking
in their sleep
burn in their dreams.

Locks on the windows
of blind glass
will not break.
I kick, my foot
shatters. I pound
and pound
with disintegrating hands.

7.

IN CASE OF FIRE
BREAK GLASS

The glass breaks
into nothing
but the fire ax
in my hands.

I look at it.

Their fingers are torches,
their heads are crowns of fire.

Instant lives cross
their faces, eaten by a fire
like age. Ecstatic
at the first touch
trying to wake them,
how soon they're lost
in the numbed wilderness
of their own skins,
frightened by the flesh
that shrinks and fails
in the hold of fire,
the fireclock.

8.
Hands that burn
wander the air. Tiny
rapid faces craze
in the heat.

My helpless eyes,
my witness heart,
which would seal shut
are open wide.

My hands, weeping and white,
tighten on the ax.

All that I am
wants to say it, the unspeakable word
that wakes the world.

The child's face
says, Please.
The child's face
says, Please
the fire hurts me.

I swing.
The child is silent.
The ax is red.
Another face
says, Please.
Another.
The ax is red.
I try
to say it, try
but the word of my heart turns
to pure fire in the air.

9.
Now
the train is quiet.
The fire is out.
My back
is to the charred
silent dark.
The ax
is gone. I left it
where my eyes
turned into mirrors
of dead glass,
where I could not leave
my hands,
my eyes,
my heart.

42

I am guilty.

I have done what I have done.

I am clothed in blood.

10.

    The train stops,
the door shoots back.
Daylight. Waiting
on the platform
stands the friend.
Above him like a hole
punched into smog
hangs the sun.
His hands fan out
in greeting. I step
down starting to tell him
as he says, "Hello."
I tell him. "Hello,"
he says, and nods.

Suddenly he's wearing
a conductor's uniform.
I tell him fire,
there's fire on board.
He stops. "Fire?
Excuse me, please."
He steps onto
the train then
off, smiling.
"So glad, so glad,
so *glad* you came."

The watch
deep in his pocket
pronounces every word.

11.

    I turn
to walk away and hear
the movements balanced
in him click and whir.
I know his hand
still agitates the air
with greeting.

This was my destination.

This was to be my home.

City asleep, city miming.
Old friends captive
to the trance of motions.
Everywhere worn tracks
criscross in the sun,
shining with promise.
Beyond the yard
streets and buildings
streaked with soot
glow with their goods.
Cinder underfoot.
Each track going somewhere
from somewhere,
each street. Each building
filled with the traffic
of habitual despair,

dreamwalkers who stare
from the wide-eyed sleep
of habitual desire.

12.
    At nightfall
I am still walking.

My shadows stretch two ways.

One is cast before me
by the last lit buildings of the city,
one is thrown behind
by prehistoric stars and the reflective moon.

13.
    I am still walking
and the wilderness behind me burns.
I am still walking
and the presence of the woods is dark ahead.
I am still walking
and the wilderness above me burns.
I am still walking
and the earth supports me where I move with care.
I am still walking
and the wilderness below me burns.
I am still walking
and the air I breathe is reborn in my lungs.
I am still walking
and the wilderness before me burns.
I am still walking.
My heart swallows its own blood.

14.

As I walk
the points of fire grow clearer
and as I walk
I hear the fire sing.

As I walk
I see with a new seeing
and as I walk
with every step I burn.

15.

I am still walking,
as I burn.

I am still walking,
a flame within the fire.

As I walk
I hear the fire singing.

As I burn
I am the fire's song.

4. Magnet of the Heart

TO WALK ACROSS

              It is the body
      that is Christ and walks
      upon the waters with perfect
      awareness as its expression
      of equivalence. And it is the
      deliberate apostles, untried,
      trained by the mind,
      who expect to walk across
      the desert of ideas
      with all the camels of desire
      in caravan behind them,
      with only words to quench
      the desert thirst. These camels,
      gaunt, tall, bloody-eyed,
      weaving on thin stalks
      of bone and shadow,
      turned carnivore
      long ago. It is the holy
      body walks uninterrupted
      across the bright waters
      of its own.

SWEAT

I.

Headlights off, the night comes on
of cows in fields, their eyes
that gave our light back
gone now: lumps
of darkness in the dark
crunching pebbles
under tall grass.

Door
wide to the lamplight, the dim faces
of strangers, brothers,
and the scent of smoke. On the walls
hides are hung—a small bear
with a hole between the ears,
two deer. From a raw post
in the center of the room,
mothlike brilliance shines
from the fanned tails
of three wild grouse.

Round stones heat
outside in a shallow pit
while we talk by the wood stove.
A hound in the far corner
snores as we strip.

II.

Into the dome through the hole
closing behind us: heat, dark,
only the glowing of the stones
as our bodies open to the heated air
that sizzles blindly up

into our faces. The scalding
presence of a handful of sage
torn from the cows' field
fills the dissolving universe.
Not me now, not you,
just darkness and the heat, a few words
from nowhere. Then nothing
but darkness, heat.
                    The entire
skin sobs with torture, pleasure
in the sizzle of steam,
the sear of sage. Darkness. Heat.
Skin has melted and muscles
soften like doeskin. Bones
surrender their rigidity and brain
gives up ideas as easily as lungs
give up the air or flesh its water,
spirit its tent of flesh.

III.

Out of the sweat lodge
of bowed willow sealed by hides
and darkness sealed in darkness,
we rush into the still water
charged by stars and frost:
bodies slam shut, scream,
duck and cry out
cries of ice, of fire.

Stars on their dark axles turn,
blood in its old bloodbed
rushes, floods. The cows of darkness

51

move toward us now
as toward a newborn calf
still glistening in the grass.

We stand up in the night,
shivering, grinning,
silent among mountainous echoes
of our helplessness
as we dunk again.

We shine, and the world
around us gives us back
our shining.

NEAR LITTLE RIVER CEMETERY

We edge down
from an inland crater's brim
toward a white beach
hidden at the bottom,
descending step by step
among ledges and mudslides,
catching at the ferns
that pull loose handhold
by handhold, hands
and faces green
and black
with ferns and muck.

At the base
heavy waters brighten
like the eyes of bulls,
blink and vanish
in the cave to the sea.
Among traces of foam
at the mouth
haloing bits of abalone
glitter and spark,
shine like sequins
from the wedding gowns
of brides, breathless once,
and settled, breathless again,
into a dark and vowless earth.

We sit in the dazzle
and stare, accidental
descendants of a rainbow
of lives worn to sand,
becalmed, willing now
to be emptyhanded and silent,
wide-aware.

ANAMAX OPEN PIT
Graveyard Shift

for Patti, heavy equipment operator

1.

Even with her engine blasting
and the lowered
scraper blade pressing
tons of rubble
through the dark,
this much is clear:
As far as she can see
on every side, farther,
the submarine light
of a full green winter moon
inundates the desert,
shines like the ocean
which shimmered here
millions of years
before these mountains rose.

Fossils lie like bookmarks
pressed among pages of stone
reciting vivid memories
of the sea into the air.
Mount Lemmon, once sacred
to the first people here,
looms brooding
above the murk
like a monstrous omen
from the dream no headlight
can expose,
no blade force.

Yet the bright arc
of her blade does force
mound upon mound of ore
as her headlights

55

catch the tips
　　　of distant saguaros.
They rise
　　alert as totems
　　　　from the desert floor.

　　　　2.
Break time.
　　She cuts the engine
and the lights
　　　and waits. Dust
falls from overhead. Orion
　　　　brightens. The desert
in the dark is luminous,
　　　　and in another corner
of the pit shovels and dozers
　　　groan and roar like
huge abyssal creatures
　　　　feeding in the circles
of their own light.

The great tire
　　　she leans against
for warmth
　　　is warm as if alive,
ridged and dusty skin
　　　　almost reptilian.
The first hot bitter breath
　　　of coffee rises
from her steel thermos
　　　and, slowly, after hours
of headlights leaching
　　　color from the rocks,

56

she sees again
    the slate blue moonlit
shades of hills and sky,
    orange and yellow glints
of stars, red and blue,
    dim aqueous green.

3.

Shock-white, quick, the flaring
meteor falls so close
she hears it hiss

as all around her
by that instant light
is shown—the ruinous geometric

wound of the pit,
the saguaros at the rim
stationed like sentinels—

before the waters of darkness
can descend upon her startled face,
extinguish the live glow of her hands.

4.

In that newly declared dark,
from some neighboring ravine
no blade has yet torn apart,
a spectral band of coyotes start
as if to call down upon earth
a whole sky full of stars,
the entire firmament of fire,
crying out their cries like prayers
to the ear of Time, which listens,
and to one woman, who hears.

THE DOLPHIN STONE

Today above the desert on a rock
rising from sand as gracefully
as a dolphin from a level sea,
we watched the late light fill
the toothed horizon yet again
as briared chaparral took darkness
from the air and snarled.

The dry wash sank and dimmed
with chill far below us
as we watched the skullbright
moon rise from a live oak,
ghost light shining on us
as the sun itself rose from the
China Sea where, flimsy and brilliant
as butterflies, the junks set sail.

THE GLASS HOUSE

1. Windows

At dusk in a glass house
above the disappearing sea,
we move in a diminished world
of rooms lit in the dark.

All day through the plate-glass walls
we watch waves and the sky alive
with rolling speckled seals
and gusts of brilliant gulls,
the occasional gleam of whales
heading south, swans heading south,
the bluff and flowing fields of grass
and clouds forming, reforming—
yet these walls of glass, at night,
can admit nothing as they mirror us
caught up in those reflections
which, willing to deny the world,
are able to deny the dark.

Late, as we give up our light
and each thing it illuminates
goes out, reflections vanish,
and the dark that houses us
clarifies the glass again
to reveal various phases
of the tidal moon, confluencies
apparent in the drift of clouds,
universal images of origin
that circulate most clearly
where reflections cease.

2. Oncoming Fog

On that bluff across the bay
rows of narrow buildings
and tall Victorian houses
pale slowly and disappear
as the cliff itself
loses definition.

Occasional lights,
like signals, flare
and fail.

While this house
goes blind, I turn
more inward hourly,
feeding as the camel
on a long dry
senseless journey feeds
from all the nourishment
it knew to store.

3. Swallow

A bird was caught in the house
and beat at the windows, hung
brushing wings and beak
against a surface clear and pitiless
as a spider's gaze. Back
and forth over our heads
it flew, frantic, dazed
by the myriad false exits.

When we tried to catch it
to set it free, it fled swooping
from us to the bright windows,
crashing and crashing, frightened
by our hands and our wide mouths
as we reached out crying
bird, bird in the open room.

Had the room been even
slightly larger, the terrified
bird stronger, smarter,
it might have escaped
to starve, snuggling glass
in the sunlit rafters. All day
it perched just out of reach
and all night in the dark beat
at the center of our dreams
until it fell, quivering
to the floor.
            I was half-awake
at dawn standing barefoot
in the doorway of the house,
certain it had been my heart
that leapt from my own
hand into the morning sun.

TEMPERANCE POEMS

1.

Iron, reddened
and plunged
shrieking into cold
water, can harden
to a temper
suitable for use
as either tool
or weapon.

2.

This is the nature
of temper: Until
the right chill
succeeds the right
passion, enduring
just as the metal's
character requires,
the ore is dross
dreaming of steel,
and dares not wake.

3.

Shunning extremes
of heat and cold,
dreading outrageous
successions
of the two,
we remain unprepared
to implement desire—
except within those
solitudes of cunning
which are the exercise
of a fool by a fool.

WHERE THERE IS NO HAND TO HOLD

Why the master must be relentless
is that some who aspire will, at last,
approach, in innocence,
abysses only a sure foothold
on an invisible stretch of gut
can cross.

        There is no hand
to hold there, no approval
once the glance down
disproves all comfort.
Praises fail on the ear tuned
by true risk, as inspiration
wells from the awed heart. Here
where even encouragement distracts,
balance is the grace to resist
every gravity opposing
focused presence,
                movement forward and alone.

SONG FROM THE SURFACE
OF THE EARTH

Overhead light stretches out a roof of silk and ice
drawing us up
drawing our eyes gradually up from thawing earth
        our turning eyes sleek as
          otters come to the surface of their pools
            through rings of slowly widening light

Earth earth you rise up too in vegetable
eyes shining from brambles and twigs
your steeples of grass emerging from the snow plains
        your weedstalks lit like candles
          urging a contagion of faith as brilliant
            as the streets of a nation long besieged and
              victorious at last

While the bones of the dead glitter in their mineral moonlight
and their voices
are mistaken for the wind
        we walk upon the surface of the earth
          alert as the awakened must be always to the shifts in
            appearance
            aware of the ungoverned fire beneath the waters
            under the earth

BLUE LAKE DREAM

1.

I float upon a lake, suspended
In my simple boat of skin.

All above me is the azure
Blazing of the inner bowl.

Below and all around
Extends the mirror, tense and blue.

I am floating on my back,
Arms spread, legs parallel, eyes wide.

2.

I am drawn swirling upward
By the vacuum of the dome,

Rushing downward by the massive depths:
Slowly on the surface I revolve

All around the great blue
Mountains of the shore

Ring me with increasing force,
Pull with power absolute

And absolutely countered
By the magnet of my heart.

Between the explosion outward
And collapse within

I am witness
To the awe of stasis,

I, who am Lodestone,
I, Brain,

I, inner Sun
Utterly ablaze in the ark of the Skull.

3.

Floating on my back I am turning
As Earth turns—flung out from the center,

Drawn in by the core—
Arms spread, eyes wide.

Eyes gone blind as stone.
Eyes made clear as diamond.

4.

In my skull grows
A light

Brighter than all the fire
Round Salamander's hull

Who sets forth through the wavering of flames
Who will not dwell in fire

Who shall pass through.

5. Feast of Light

SONG OF AN EYE'S OPENING

The small bow of color taken
into the vanishing wave
slides back across sand,
rests at my feet. In my
hand it becomes a disc
of abalone in a hand
I've never seen before.

In the mask of flesh
that supports the shining
mask of shell, the mute bones
are suddenly articulate,
poised with a grace not mine
—Then my palm becomes
a face with a rainbow eye
opening in it, opening
as my own eyes uncontrollably
close to its gaze; it disappears,
restoring to my human hand
the bright inhuman glow.

SONG OF A HAWK'S GLANCE

Bits of the moon
glint from the hawk's
broad skull, wavering
a snake's length
from my face. The sky
falls back so deeply
it disappears as
water disappears
around a diver's skin.

This is the cliff's edge
where wind has delivered me
this hawk, adrift
with hunger and buoyant
in a freefall
through these currencies
I breathe
as they breathe me:
Outcries and inspirations
of an earth abrupt
as hawk and sky, sea
and cloudflow, all quick
margins of expanse.

SONG OF THE PIPER

—for Bruce

I have gone out on the bluffs at dusk
where a piper pipers the sun down,
and I've remained to hear the pibroch
of late quarreling gulls
indifferent to this cold contest
of sea and disintegrating stone,
yet avid for those crumbs of fish
that flash to dust if one rock falls.

SONG OF SALT AND THE GALE

Arched waves hit the rocks
and arc up cliffs
like flame, and flecks
of spume blown inland
on the pale level wind
speckle the wild carrots
and the grass.
                    Here
slow cloudlike sheep and mares
with colts on stilts
and does attending
sky-eyed fawns
gather along the sea
at dawn, licking and grazing
where odors of spindrift
rise like sunlight from a living dew.

SONG OF THE WINDWALKER

Wind walks behind
caressing the back
of my head, parting
grass in the fields
and my hair.
    I love her
lifting hawks and gulls,
inspiring foxes, quail,
reforming the horizon
with her hands, pushing
as I sail before her
laughing, moved clear
of my dark mood
by one careless brush
with this brighthaired
sister of my breath.

SONG OF THE DAWNCOCK

—for Lilo

The cock on the icebright post wakes, gazes
with his two-pronged glance
   east, west.

Feet of horn locked in a blaze of frost
gradually discharging the glitter of stars
   and glow of the moon,
hook of a head cocked back,
he cries into the dark one lucent cry.

He rattles the harsh rainbow of his mane.

SONG OF LEVELS

Each wave
driven cliffward
blasts to foam
against the rocks,
consumes the gnarling
roots of trees
whose upper branches
vanish into mist.

Below the waves
glide creatures
feeding and serene.

Above mist
shines the daystar,
constant in oceanic air.

SONG ALTERING ALL

A bird lies on the ground.

Ignore the bird.
        Think
rather of the quail-like
qualities of the ruffled
earth it is given to,
the grouse-like thrumming
of leaves in the trees
at dusk, the flash
of flamingo at sunset.
If even in the dark
you are given to irony,
consider that now
the worm
gets the late bird.

And by dawnlight
review the sky,
wide clear eye
which, seeing all things,
regards none.

The birdlike daylight
whose song
alters everything and yet
is nothing.

Birdlike.

Birdlike.

Birdlike.

LITTLE SONG OF PATIENCE

> When grass enters the houses
> the hearts of my people shall rejoice.
> —Isaiah

Wall is
> held to wall
to wall
> by roof alone

When the
> roof caves in
all walls
> will collapse

Now everything
> that tries
to haunt
> the house

must haunt
> wide air
and disappear
> in that expanse

Grass will grow
birds will sing
in the open square
walls used to ring

SONG OF THE CONSOLATION

Eye, you perch in the cave's mouth balancing
    one darkness with all the light.
Ear, you convey to the steady blood indifferent
    blessings of the sea.
Flesh, sensual white frontier, you poise rapt
    between urgency and the holy orbits of sleep.

    What is consolable already has consolation.

My own chosen weddings, hour upon hour,
Pass like darkness over snow as it melts and flows
Taking the sun and the moon to its center, shining,
Taking the inseparable stars one by one by one.

    What is consolable already has consolation.

What is consolable already knows its motions,
Practices its tides as the ocean slides over
    this earth
Charged with seed as waters are charged with the
    flashing of fishes.
Moon, you glitter the edges of waves, glow from
    the turned faces of the grass.

    What is consolable already has consolation.

My own bones luminous in my flesh beat like a clock
—With whom may I share this unendurable fire,
This feast of light I am devoured by and devour?
Darkness moves over snow, and the shining remains.

    What is consolable already has consolation.

SONG

0
The slender brilliance of flutes
flesh must fall from
before the bones may play

&
the open skull years have healed
to hold all currents of the mind
soon shall hold the thoughtless rain

&
such sweet energy wraps these parts
breeding out of dreams and hunger
all the beauty I can bear

Let all birds feast on the poet laid to rest then sing!

TO BUILD A HOUSE UPON THE ROCK

Dry words are for building
on dry sand.
    Who would build
a house upon the rock
must leave
the mountain quarry
and learn to gather boulders from the air.

PITT POETRY SERIES
Ed Ochester, General Editor